USEFUL EXPRESSIONS

in FRENCH

FOR THE ENGLISH–SPEAKING TOURIST

Editors: A. Z. Stern — Joseph A. Reif, Ph.D.

·K·U·P·E·R·A

© 1991 KS-JM Books

Distributed in the United Kingdom by:
Kuperard (London) Ltd.
30 Cliff Road
London NW1 9AG

ISBN 1-870668-67-7

All rights reserved. No part of this book may be reproduced or transmitted in any form or by any means, electronic or mechanical, including photocopying, recording or by any information storage and retrieval system without permission in writing from the publisher.

This booklet is an up-to-date and practical phrase book for your trip to a French-speaking country. It includes the phrases and vocabulary you will need in most of the situations in which you will find yourself, and it contains a pronunciation guide for all the material. Some of the phrases occur in more than one section so that you do not have to turn pages back and forth. At the beginning is a basic, general vocabulary with which you should become familiar, and at the end is a list of emergency expressions for quick reference.

The pronunciation of French differs from English particularly in the vowels sounds and in the rhythm of speech. The transcription, when read as if it were English, will give a close approximation to normal French pronunciation. All syllables should be given equal stress with the last syllable a bit longer than the rest. Special attention should be paid to the following vowel sounds:

ew is pronounced like **ee**, but with rounded lips.

The nasal sounds **ahn, ehn, óhn, uhn** should be pronounced as though they were followed by a very weak **k** sound: **ahn(k), ehn(k), ohn(k), uhn(k).**

The consonants in the transcription are read as in English with the following exceptions:

g as in **g**o (not as in **g**entle)

r is pronounced with friction in the back of the mouth.

zh is pronounced like the **g** in beige or the **s** in measure.

CONTENTS

Basic Dictionary	1	Airplane	39
First meeting, Greetings	10	Car journey	41
Hotel	12	Signs	44
Information at hotel	16	Garage	47
Taxi	19	Repairs	48
In the post office	19	Parts of a car	50
In the restaurant	22	Physicians	51
Grocery	26	Types of doctors	51
Fruits and vegetables	27	Illnesses	52
Bank	29	Parts of the body	53
Clothes	30	Pharmacy	55
Colors	33	Time	56
Laundry	33	Days of the week	57
At the hairdresser	34	Months	58
Bookshop	35	Seasons	58
Weather	36	Numbers	58
Transport	37	Emergency expressions	60
Train, Bus	37		

BASIC DICTIONARY	**VOCABULAIRE DE BASE**	**VO-KA-BEW-LEHR DE BAZ**
Thank you	Merci	mehr-see
Thank you very much	Merci beaucoup	mehr-see boh-koo
Please	S'il vous plaît	seel-voo-pleh
Excuse me	Excusez-moi	ex-kew-zay mwah
Never mind	De rien	de ree-ehn
What? What is that?	Quoi? Qu'est-ce que c'est?	kwah? kess-ke-seh?
Where? Where is that?	Où? Où est ca?	oo? oo-eh-sah?
When? How?	Quand? Comment?	kahn? kom-mahn
Which? Why?	Lequel? Pourquoi?	le-kel? poor-kwah?
Is that?	Est-ce que c'est...?	ess-ke-seh...?
That is not	Ce n'est pas...	se-neh-pah...
Yes, no, perhaps	Oui, non, peut-être	wee, nohn, per-tetr
Correct, incorrect	Correct, incorrect	korrekt, ehn-ko-rekt
So so	Comme-ci comme-ca	kom-see kom-sah
Good, bad	Bon, mauvais	bohn, moh-veh
Not good, not bad	Pas bon, pas mauvais	pah-bohn, pah-moh-veh
There is, there is not	Il y a, il n'y a pas	ee-lee-ah, eel-nee-ah-pah

I, you (m.s.) (f.s.)	Je, vous	zhe, voo
He, she	Il, elle	eel, el
We	Nous	noo
you (m. pl.), (f. pl.)	Vous	voo
They	Ils(m), elles(f)	eel, el
Mine, yours	Le mien, le vôtre	le-mee-ehn, le-voh-tr
Ours, theirs	Le nôtre, le leur	le-noh-tr, le-lerr
At my place, at your place	Chez-moi, chez-vous	shay-mwah, shay-voo
Wet, dry	Mouillé, sec	moo-ee-yay, seck
Old, new	Ancien, nouveau	ahn-see-ehn, noo-voh
Pretty, not nice	Joli, pas joli	zho-lee, pas-zho-lee
Much, few	Beaucoup, peu	boh-koo, per
How many? How much?	Combien?	kohn-byehn?
Cheap, expensive	À bon marché, cher	ah-bohn-mar-shay, shehr
Very expensive	Très cher	treh-shehr
Free (of charge)	Gratis	gra-teess
More, less	Plus, moins	plew, mwehn
Cheaper	À meilleur marché	ah-may-yerr-mar-shay
more expensive	plus cher	plew shehr

Heavy, light	Lourd, léger	loor, lay-zhay
Now, at the same time as...	Maintenant, au moment même où...	mehn-te-nahn, oh-mo-mahn-mem-oo
During	Pendant	pahn-dahn
Early, late	De bonne heure, en retard	de-bon-nerr, ahn-re-tahr
On time, in time	À l'heure	ah-lerr
Here, there	Ici, là bas	ee-see, lah-bah
Inside, outside	Dedans, dehors	de-dahn, de-or
Up (stairs), down (stairs)	En haut, en bas	ahn oh, ahn bah
To...	A	ah
Near, far	Proche, loin	prosh, lwehn
In front of	Devant	de-vahn
Behind, after	Derrière, après	dehr-yehr, ah-preh
Sky	Ciel	see-el
Sun, moon	Soleil, lune	so-lay, lewn
Stars	Étoiles	ay-twahl
Light, darkness	Lumière, ténebres	lew-myehr, tay-nebr
Heat, cold, warm	Chaleur, froid, tiède	shah-lerr, frwah, tyed

East, west	Est, ouest	est, west
North, south	Nord, sud	nor, syewd
Rain, snow, wind	Pluie, neige, vent	plwee, nezh, vahn
Earth, mountain, valley	Terre, montagne, vallée	tehr, mohn-tann-ye, val-lay
River, bridge	Fleuve, pont	flerv, pohn
Desert, sand	Désert, sable	day-zehr, sah-bl
Sea, water, ship	Mer, eau, bateau	mehr, oh, bah-toh
Country, place	Place, pays	plass, peh-ee
City, village	Ville, village	veel, vee-lazh
Road, street	Route, rue	root, rew
House, flat	Maison, appartement	meh-zohn, ah-par-te-mahn
Room, door	Chambre, porte	shahn-br, port
Key, lock	Clé, serrure	klay, seh-rewr
Wall, window	Mur, fenêtre	mewr, fe-neh-tr
Roof, steps	Toit, escalier	twah, es-kal-yay
Kitchen	Cuisine	kwee-zeen
Toilet	Toilettes (w.c.)	twah-let (vay-say)
Bed, pillows	Lit, oreillers	lee, or-ray-yay

Blanket, carpet	Couverture, tapis	koo-vehr-tewr, tah-pee
Table, chair	Table, chaise	tah-bl, shehz
Man, woman	Homme, femme	om, fam
Father, mother	Père, mère	pehr, mehr
Son, daughter	Fils, fille	fees, fee
Grandson, granddaughter	Petit-fils, Petite-fille	pe-tee-fees, pe-teet-fee
Brother, sister	Frère, soeur	frehr, serr
Uncle, aunt	Oncle, tante	ohn-kl, tahnt
Husband, wife	Mari, femme	mah-ree, fam
Boy, girl	Garcon, jeune fille	gar-sohn, zhern-fee
Old man, old woman	Vieux, vieille	vee-er, vee-ay
To want	Vouloir	vool-wahr
I want, you want	Je veux, vous voulez	zhe ver, voo voo-lay
I wanted, you wanted	Je voulais, vous vouliez	zhe voo-leh, voo vool-yay
I will want, you will want	Je voudrai, vous voudrez	zhe vood-ray, voo vood-ray
I do not want	Je ne veux pas	zhe ne ver pah
To visit	Visiter	vee-zee-tay
I visit, you visit	Je visite, vous visitez	zhe vee-zeet, voo vee-zee-tay

I visited, you visited	J'ai visité, vous avez visité	zhay vee-zee-tay, voo-zah-vay vee-zee-tay
I will visit, you will visit	Je visiterai, vous visiterez	zhe vee-zee-tray, voo vee-zee-tray
To speak	Parler	par-lay
I speak, you speak	Je parle, vous parlez	zhe parl, voo par-lay
I spoke, you spoke	J'ai parlé, vous avez parlez	zhay par-lay, voo-zah-vay par-lay
I will speak, you will speak	Je parlerais, vous parlerais	zhe par-le-ray, voo par-le-ray
I do not speak	Je ne parle pas	zhe ne parl pah
To understand	Comprendre	kohn-prahn-dr
I understand, you understand	Je comprends, vous comprenez	zhe kohn-prahn, voo kohn-pre-nay
I understood, you understood	J'au compris, vous avez compris	zhay kohn-pree, voo-zah-vay kohn-pree
I do not understand	Je ne comprends pas	zhe ne kohn-prahn pah
To go	Aller	ah-lay
I go, you go	Je vais, vous allez	zhe veh, voo-zah-lay

I went, you went	Je suis allé, vous êtes allés	zhe swee-zah-lay, voo-zet-zah-lay
I will go, you will go	J'irai, vous irez	zhee-ray, voo-zee-ray
I do not go	Je ne vais pas	zhe ne veh pah
To travel	Voyager	vwah-yah-zhay
I travel, you travel	Je voyage, vous voyagez	zhe-vwah-yazh, voo vwah-yah-zhay
I travelled, you travelled	J'ai voyagé, vous avez voyagé	zhay vwah-yah-zhay, voo-zah-vay vwah-yah-zhay
I will travel, you will travel	Je voyagerai, vous voyagerez	zhe vwah-yazh-ray, voo vwah-yazh-ray
I do not travel	Je ne voyage pas	zhe ne vwah-yazh pah
To sleep	Dormir	dor-meer
I sleep, you sleep	Je dors, vous dormez	zhe dor, voo dor-may
I slept, you slept	Je dormais, vous dormiez	zhe dor-meh, voo dorm-yay
I will sleep	Je dormirai	zhe dor-mee-ray
You will sleep	Vous dormirez	voo dor-mee-ray
I do not sleep	Je ne dors pas	zhe ne dor pah

I rest, you rest	Je me repose, vous vous reposez	zhe me re-pohz, voo voo re-poh-zay
I rested, you rested	Je me suis reposé, vous vous êtes reposés	zhe-me-swee re-poh-zay, voo-voo-zet re-poh-zay
I will rest, you will rest	Je me reposerai, vous vous reposerez	zhe me re-pohz-ray, voo voo re-pohz-ray
I do not rest	Je ne me repose pas	zhe ne me re-pohz pah
To eat	Manger	mahn-zhay
I eat, you eat	Je mange, vous mangez	zhe mahnzh, voo mahn-zhay
I ate, you ate	J'ai mangé, vous avez mangé	zhay mahn-zhay, voo-zah-vay mahn-zhay
I will eat, you will eat	Je mangerai, vous mangerez	zhe mahn-zhe-ray, voo mahn-zhe-ray
I do not eat	Je ne mange pas	zhe ne mahnzh pah
To drink	Boire	bwahr
I drink, you drink	Je bois, vous buvez	zhe bwah, voo bew-vay
I drank, you drank	J'ai bu, vous avez bu	zhay bew, voo-zah-vay bew
I will drink, you will drink	Je boirai, vous boirez	zhe bwah-ray, voo bwah-ray

I do not drink	Je ne bois pas	zhe ne bwah pah
I am afraid, you are afraid	J'ai peur, vous avez peur	zhay perr, voo-zah-vay perr
I was afraid, you were afraid	J'avais peur, vous aviez peur	zhah-veh perr, voo-zah-vyay perr
I am not afraid	Je n'ai pas peur	zhe nay pah perr
I am in a hurry	Je me presse	zhe me press
I hurried	J'étais pressé	zhay-teh press-say
I am not in a hurry	Je ne me presse pas	zhe ne me press pah
I need help	J'ai besoin de l'aide	zhay be-zwehn delehd
I asked for help	J'ai demandé de l'aide	zhay de-mahn-day delehd
I do not need help	Je n'ai pas besoin d'aide	zhe nay pah be-zwehn dehd
Passport	Passeport	pass-por
Flight, flight number…	Vol, vol numéro…	vol, vol new-may-roh…
Outgoing flight	Départ…	day-par
Following flight	Le prochain vol	le pro-shehn vol
Suitcase	Bageges	ba-gazh
Customs, money	Douane, argent	doo-ann, ar-zhahn

FIRST MEETING; GREETINGS	**PREMIÉRE RENCONTRE; SALUTATIONS**	**PRE-MEE-EHR RAHN-KOHN-TRE; SA-LEW-TA-SYOHN**
Hello!	Bon jour!	bohn zhoor!
Good morning	Bon jour	bohn zhoor
Good evening	Bon soir	bohn swahr
Good night	Bon soir	bohn swahr
Welcome!	Bienvenu!	byehn-ve-new!
My name is ...	Je m'âppelle	zhe ma-pel
I come from England	Je viens d'Angleterre	zhe vyehn dahn-gle-tehr
I am from the United-States	Je viens des Etats-Unis	zhe vyehn day-zay-tah-zew-nee
I speak English	Je parle anglais	zhe parl ahn-gleh
I am pleased to meet you	Enchanté de faire votre connaissance	zhn-shahn-tay de fehr votr ko-nes-sahn-ss
How are you?	Comment allez-vous?	ko-mahn-ta-lay-voo?
Fine, thank you,	Trés bien, merci	treh byehn, mehr-see
All right	Tout va bien	too vah byehn

Is there someone here who speaks English?	Y a-t-il ici quelqu'un qui parle l'anglais?	ee-a-teel ee-see kel-kuhn kee parl lahn-gleh?
Yes, no	Oui, non	wee; nohn
I don't speak French	Je ne parle pas français	zhe ne parl pah frahn-seh
I speak only English	Je ne parle qu'anglais	zhe ne parl kahn-gleh
I speak a little	Je parle un peu	zhe parl uhn per
Do you understand me?	Me comprenez-vous?	me kohn-pre-nay-voo?
I understand a little	Je comprends un peu	zhe khon-prahn uhn per
Pardon, excuse me	Pardon, excusez-moi	par-dohn; ex-kew-zay-mwah
I am sorry	Je m'excuse	zhe mex-kewz
It doesn't matter	Cela ne fait rien	se-la ne feh ryehn
Thank you very much	Merci beaucoup	mer-see boh-koo
What do you want?	Que désirez-vous	ke day-zee-ray-voo?
I would like to visit the city	Je voudrais aller en ville	zhe vood-reh a-lay ahn veel
Thank you for your attention	Merci pour votre attention	mehr-see poor votr a-tahn-syohn
Good luck!	Bon chance!	bohn shahn-ss!
Goodbye!	Au revoir!	oh-re-vwahr!

HOTEL	**À L'HÔTEL**	**AH LOH-TEL**
I am looking for a good hotel	Je cherche un bon hôtel	zhe shersh uhn bohn-oh-tel
I am looking for an inexpensive hotel	Je cherche un hôtel pas cher	zhe shersh uhn oh-tel pah-shehr
I booked a room here, is it ready?	J'ai réservé une chambre. Est-elle prête?	zhay ray-zehr-vay ewn shahn-br. eh-tel pret?
Have you a single room? A double room?	Avez-vous une chambre pour une personne? pour un couple?	a-vay-voo ewn shahn-br poor ewn per-son? poor uhn koopl?
Have you a better room?	Avez-vous une meilleure chambre?	a-vay-voo ewn may-yerr shahn-br?
Is the room air-conditioned?	Y a-t-il l'air conditionné dans la chambre?	ee-a-teel lehr kohn-dee-syon-nay dahn la shahn-br?
Does the room have a shower?	Y a-t-il une douche dans la chambre?	ee-a-teel ewn doosh dahn la shahn-br?
With breakfast?	Avec le petit déjeuner?	a-veck le-pe-tee day-zher-nay?
How much is the room?	Quel est le prix de la chambre?	kel-eh le pree de la shahn-br?

I would like to see the room	Je voudrais voir la chambre	zhe vood-reh vwahr la shahn-br
Do you have something bigger?	Avez-vous une chambre plus grande?	a-vay-voo ewn shahn-br plew grahnd?
Smaller?	une chambre plus petite?	ewn shahn-br plew pe-teet?
Cheaper?	une chambre moins chère?	ewn shahn-br mwehn shehr?
Quieter?	une chambre plus tranquille?	ewn shahn-br plew trahn-kee?
Will you send for my bags?	Peux-t-on faire monter mes bagages?	perr-tohn fehr mohn-tay may ba-gazh?
I would like to keep this in the safe	Je voudrais garder ceci dans un coffre-fort	zhe vood-reh gar-day se-see dahn-zuhn koff-re-for
Where is the ladies room?	Où se trouvent les toilettes pour dames?	oo-se-troov lay twah-let poor dam?
Where is the men's room?	Où se trouvent les toilettes pour hommes?	oo-se-troov lay twah-let poor-omm?
Where is the dining room?	Où se trouve la salle à manger?	oo-se-troov la sahl-a-mahn-zhay?

Please, wake me at ...	Reveillez-moi à ... s'il vous plaît	re-vay-yay-mwah ah ... seel-voo-pleh
Who's there? Please wait!	Qui est là? Attendez, s'il vous plaît!	kee-eh-lah? ah-tahn-day seel-voo-pleh!
Come in!	Entrez!	ahn-tray!
May I have another towel?	Est-ce que je peux recevoir une serviette de plus?	ess-ke-zhe-perr re-se-vwahr ewn sehr-vee-yet de-plew-ss?
May I have another pillow?	Est-ce que je peux recevoir un oreiller de plus?	ess-ke-zhe-perr re-se-vwahr uhn-or-ray-yay de-plew-ss?
...another blanket?	...une couverture de plus?	...ewn koo-vehr-tewr de-plew-ss?
...hangers?	...des cintres	...day sehn-tr
...hot water bottle?	...une bouillotte	...ewn boo-yott
...night lamp?	...une lampe de chevet	...ewn lahmp de she-veh
...needle and thread?	...une aiguille et du fil	...ewn eh-gwee ay dew feel?
...writing paper? pen?	...de papier à letters, un stylo	...de pap-yay ah-let-tr, uhn stee-loh

English	French	Pronunciation
Could you cable abroad for me?	Pourriez-vous m'envoyer un télégramme à l'étranger?	poo-ree-ay-voo mahn-vwah-yay uhn tay-lay-gram ah lay-trahn-zhay?
A vacant room	Une chambre vacante	ewn shahn-br va-kahnt
Receptionist	Le réceptioniste	le ray-sep-syohn-neest
Chambermaid	La femme de chambre	la fam de shahn-br
Security Officer	L'officier de sécurité	lo-fees-yay de say-kew-ree-tay
Waiter	Le serveur	le ser-verr
Dining Room	La salle à manger	la sahl ah-mahn-zhay
Reception Room	La réception	la ray-sep-syohn
Lift boy (Elevator Boy)	Le liftier	le leef-tyay
Room key	La clé de la chambre	la klay de la shahn-br
Room number	Le numéro de la chambre	le new-may-roh de la shahn-br
Bed, Blanket	Lit, couverture	lee, koo-vehr-tewr
Sheet	Drap	drah
Men's toilet, Ladies' toilet	Toilettes pour hommes, Toilettes pour dames	twah-let poor-om, twah-let poor dam
Toilet paper	Papier hygiénique	pap-yay ee-zhee-ay-neek

INFORMATION AT HOTEL	RENSEIGNEMENTS REÇUS À L'HÔTEL	RAHN-SEN-MAHN RE-SYEW AH-LOH–TEL
Is there a taxi station nearby?	Y a-t-il une station de taxis toute proche?	ee-a-teel ewn sta-syohn de taxi toot prosh?
What is the telephone number?	Quel est son numéro de téléphone?	kel eh sohn new-may-roh de-tay-lay-fonn?
How do I get to ...?	Comment arrive-t-on à ...	ko-mahn ah-reev-tohn ah...?
By bus? Where is the bus stop?	En autobus? Où se trouve la station d'autobus?	ahn-oh-toh-bew-ss? oo-se-troov la sta-syohn doh-toh-bew-ss?
Where is the nearest post office?	Où se trouve le bureau de poste le plus proche?	oo-se-troov le-bew-roh de-post le plew prosh?
Ladies' hairdresser	Salon de coiffure pour dames	sah-lohn de kwah-fewr poor dam
Barber	Salon de coiffure pour hommes	sah-lohn de kwah-fewr poor-om
Laundry	Blanchisserie	blahn-shee-se-ree
Shop	Magasin	mah-gah-zehn

Where can I get a snack?	Où puis-je recevoir un casse-croûte?	oo-pweezh re-se-vwahr uhn kass-kroot?
Is there a grocery nearby?	Y a-t-il une épicerie tout proche?	ee-a-teel ewn ay-pee-se-ree too-prosh?
Where is the Tourist Information Office?	Où se trouve le bureau d'information pour touristes?	oo-se-troov le bew-roh dehn-for-ma-syohn poor too-reest?
Can I have a programme of this week's events?	Puis-je recevoir le programme des spectacles pour cette semaine?	pweezh re-se-vwahr le pro-gram day spek-takl poor set se-men?
How can I get to …?	Comment arrive-t-on à …?	ko-mahn ah-reev-tohn ah…?
…on foot?	…á pied?	…ah-pyay?
…by bus?	…en autobus?	…ahn-oh-toh-bew-ss?
…to this address?	…à cette adresse?	…ah set-ad-ress?
…to the center of town?	…au centre de la ville?	…oh sahn-tr de-la-veel?
…to the shopping district?	…au centre commercial?	…oh sahn-tr ko-mehr-see-yahl?
…to a bookshop?	…à une librairie?	…ah ewn leeb-reh-ree?
…to the market?	…au marché?	…oh mar-shay?

…to the exhibition?	…à l'exposition?	…ah lex-po-zee-syohn?
…to the museum?	…au musée?	…oh mew-zay
…to the theatre?	…au théâtre?	…oh tay-atr?
…to the cinema?	…au cinema?	…oh see-nay-mah?
…to a nightclub?	…à la boîte de nuit?	…ah la-bwaht de nwee?
Which films worth seeing are on this week?	Quels filmes valent la peine d'être vus cette semaine?	kel feelm vahl la-pen deh-tr vew set-se-men?
Have you got any mail for me?	Ai-je reçu du courrier?	ehzh re-syew dew koo-ree-ay?
Is there a message for me?	Ai-je reçu un message?	ehzh re-syew uhn mes-sahzh?
I am going out and will return at …	Je sors et reviendrai à …	zhe sor ay re-vyehn-dray ah …
I'll leave the hotel tomorrow at …	Je quitterai l'hôtel demain à…	zhe keet-ray loh-tel de-mehn ah …
Please make up my bill	Préparez l'addition, s'il vous plaît	pray-pa-ray la-dee-syohn, seel-voo-pleh
May I store my luggage here until …?	Puis-je laisser mes bagages ici jusqu'à …	pweezh leh-say may ba-gahzh ee-see zhew-skah …
Goodbye (See you soon)	Au revoir (À tout à l'heure)	oh-re-vwahr (ah-too-tah-lerr)

TAXI

Please call me a taxi

Driver, would you please bring my suitcase inside?

Take me to this address, please ...

How much is the fare?

Can you come here at ... in order to take me back?

TAXI

Veuillez m'appeler un taxi

Chauffeur, veuillez m'aider à mettre la valise

Veuillez me conduire à cette adresse?

Combien dois-je payer?

Pouvez-vous revenir me chercher à ...?

TAXI

verr-yay map-lay uhn tak-see

shoh-ferr, verr-yay meh-day ah meh-tr la vah-leez

verr-yay me kohn-dweer ah set ad-ress

kohn-byehn dwahzh peh-yay?

poo-vay-voo re-ve-neer me shehr-shay ah ...

IN THE POST OFFICE

Where is the post office?

Where can I send an overseas cable?

AU BUREAU DE POSTE

Où se trouve le bureau de poste?

Où puis-je envoyer un télégramme à l'étranger?

OH BEW-ROH DE POST

oo-se-troov le bew-roh de post?

oo pweezh ahn-vwah-yay uhn tay-lay-gram ah lay-trahn-zhay?

Please, give me an overseas cable form	Je voudrais un formulaire pour un télégramme à l'étranger	zhe vood-reh uhn for-mew-lehr poor uhn tay-lay-gram ah lay-trahn-zhay
Have I written the telegram clearly?	Ai-je écrit le télégramme clairement?	ezh-ay-kree le tay-lay-gram klehr-mahn?
When will the telegram arrive?	Quand le télégramme arrivera-t-il?	kahn le tay-lay-gram ah-reev-rah-teel?
How much do I have to pay?	Combien dois-je payer?	kohn-byehn dwahzh peh-yay?
What stamps do I need for this letter by ordinary mail?	Combien de timbres faut-il pour affranchir une lettre?	kohn-byehn de tehm-br foh-teel poor ah-frahn-sheer ewn let-tr?
...by air mail?	...par avion?	...par ah-vyohn?
...by registered mail?	...recommandée?	...re-kom-mahn-day?
...by express delivery?	...express?	...ex-press?
Please send this by registered mail	Veuillez l'expédier par poste recommandée	verr-yay lex-pay-dyay par post re-kom-mahn-day
Please give me... postcards to send locally.	Donnez-moi ... cartes postales à envoyer dans le pays, s'il vous plaît	don-nay-mwah...kart poh-stal ah ahn-vwah-yay dahn le peh-ee, seel-voo-pleh

Give me airletters to America, please	Donnez-moi des aérogrammes pour l'Amérique, s'il vous plaît	don-nay-mwah day-zah-ay-roh-gram poor la-meh-reek, seel-voo-pleh
Where is the nearest post box?	Où se trouve la boîte postale la plus proche?	oo-se-troov la bwaht po-stahl la plew prosh?
May I have some telephone tokens, please?	Je voudrais des jetons de téléphone	zhe vood-reh day zhe-tohn de tay-lay-fon
Please, could you get me this number, as I could not get it by dialing?	Pourriez-vous joindre ce numéro pour moi parce que je n'ai pas réussi à le composer	poo-ree-ay-voo zhwehn-dr se new-may-roh poor mwah par-ske zhe nay-pah ray-yew-see ah la kohn-poh-zay
Please, could you put me through to the International Exchange for this number?	Je voudrais joindre ce numéro à l'étranger	zhe vood-reh zhwehn-dr se new-may-roh ah lay-trahn-zhay
Please book me a call for tomorrow at ...	Veuillez me reserver une communication pour demain à ...	verr-yay me re-zer-vay ewn kom-mew-nee-ka-syohn poor de-mehn ah ...
Please, may I have a receipt?	Puis-je recevoir un reçu?	pweezh re-se-vwahr uhn re-syew?

IN THE RESTAURANT	**AU RESTAURANT**	**OH RES-TOR-RAHN**
I am hungry	J'ai faim	zhay fehn
I am thirsty	J'ai soif	zhay swahf
Where is there a good restaurant?	Où peut-on trouver un bon restaurant?	oo perr-tohn troo-vay uhn bohn res-tor-rahn?
Waiter	Garçon	gar-sohn
Waitress	Serveuse	sehr-verz
Can I see the menu?	Puis-je voir le menu?	pweezh vwahr le me-new?
Breakfast	Petit déjeuner	pe-tee day-zherr-nay
Lunch	Déjeuner	day-zherr-nay
Dinner	Dîner	dee-nay
I would like to order	Je voudrais commander	zhe vood-reh kom-mahn-day
Give me this	Donnez-moi ça	don-nay-mwah sah
Tea with lemon, tea with milk	Thé au citron, thé au lait	tay oh see-trohn, tay oh leh
Coffee and milk, Turkish coffee	Café au lait, café turque	ka-fay oh leh, ka-fay tewrk

Milk, cocoa, espresso	Lait, chocolat, espresso	leh, sho-ko-lah, es-press-oh
Cold, warm, hot	Froid, tiède, chaud	frwah, tyehd, shoh
Cold water, soda water	De l'eau chaude, de l'eau gazeuse	de loh shohd, de-loh gah-zerz
Orange juice, grapefruit juice	Jus d'orange, jus de pamplemousse	zhew dor-rahnzh, zhew de pahn-pl-moo-ss
Cake, ice-cream	Gâteau, glace	gah-toh, glass
White beer, black beer	Bière blonde, bière brune	byehr blohnd, byehr brewn
Sweet wine, dry wine	Vin sucré, vin sec	vehn syew-kray, vehn seck
Cognac, whisky, arak	Cognac, whisky, anisette	kon-yahk, vis-kee, ah-nee-zet
Buttered roll, roll and margarine	Petit pain au beurre, petit pain à la margarine	pe-tee pehn oh berr, pe-tee pehn ah la mar-gah-reen
White bread, black bread	Pain blanc, pain noir	pehn blahn, pehn nwahr
Toast and jam	Toast à la confiture	toast ah la kohn-fee-tewr
Rolls, beigel	Petits pains, beiguel	pe-tee pehn, bay-gel
Egg, soft-boiled egg	Oeuf, oeuf à la coque	errf, errf ah la kok
Omelette, fried egg	Omelette, oeuf sur le plat	om-let, errf sewr le plah

White cheese, yellow cheese	Fromage blanc, fromage	fro-mahzh blahn, fro-mahzh
Yogurt, sour-cream	Yaourt, yoghourt, lait caillé	yah-oort, yo-goort, leh kah-yay
Sausage, hot dogs	Saucisson, Saucisses	soh-see-sohn, soh-see-ss
Vegetable salad	Macédoine de légumes	mah-say-dwahnn de lay-gewm
Salt, oil, sugar	Sel, huile, sucre	sel, weel, syew-kr
Pepper, lemon juice	Poivre, jus de citron	pwah-vr, zhew de see-trohn
Olives, pickled cucumber	Olives, cornichon	o-leev, kor-nee-shohn
Herring, pickled fish	Hareng, poisson mariné	ah-rahn, pwah-sohn mah-ree-nay
Smoked fish	Poisson fumé	pwah-sohn few-may
Filleted fish	filets de poisson	fee-leh de pwah-sohn
Baked, filled carp	Cuit, poisson farci	kwee, pwah-sohn far-see
Baked, grilled, boiled	Cuit, grillé, bouilli	kwee, gree-lay, boo-yee
Fried, steamed	Frit, Cuit à la vapeur	free, kwee ah la vah-perr
Chicken, turkey, duck	Poulet, dindon, canard	poo-leh, dehn-dohn, kah-nahr
Beef	Viande de boeuf	vee-ahnd de berf
Lamb	Viande d'agneau	vee-ahnd dan-yoh

Liver, tongue	Foie, langue	fwah, lahng
Steak, shnitzel	Steak, escalope	steak, ess-kah-lop
Meat balls	Boulettes	boo-let
Beans soup	Soupe de haricots	soop de ah-ree-koh
Vegetable soup	Soupe aux légumes	soop oh lay-gewm
Chicken soup	Bouillon de poulet	boo-ee-yohn de poo-leh
Meat soup	Bouillon de boeuf	boo-ee-yohn de berf
Mashed potatoes	Purée de pommes de terre	pew-ray de pom-de-tehr
Chips	Pommes de terre frites	pom-de-tehr freet
Fruit salad	Macédoine de fruits	mah-say-dwahn de frwee
Pudding, Bavaria cream	Pudding, crème bavaroise	pudding, krem bah-vahr-wahz
Glass, bottle, cup	Verre, bouteille, tasse	vehr, boo-tay, tass
Spoon, fork, knife	Cuillère, fourchette, couteau	kwee-yay, foor-shet, koo-toh
Plate, teaspoon	Assiette, cuillère à café	ass-yet, kwee-yehr ah kah-fay
Serviette, ashtray	Serviette, cendrier	ser-vyet, sahn-dree-ay
Toothpicks	Cure-dents	kewr-dahn
How much must I pay?	Combien vous dois-je?	kohm-byehn voo dwahzh?
Change and a receipt, please	La monnaie et un reçu, s'il vous plaît	la mon-neh ay uhn re-syew, seel-voo-pleh

GROCERY	**À L'EPICERIE**	**AH LAY-PEE-SE-REE**
White bread, brown bread	Pain blanc, pain noir	pehn blahn, pehn nwahr
Milk, yogurt	Lait, Yaourt, yoghourt	leh, yah-oort, yo-goort
Sour cream, white cheese	Créme caillée, frommage blanc	krem kah-yay, fro-mahzh blahn
Yellow cheese, salt cheese	Fromage, fromage salé	fro-mahzh, fro-mahzh sah-lay
Butter, margarine, oil	Beurre, margarine, huile	berr, mar-gah-reen, weel
Sardines, tuna fish, tuna salad	Sardines, thon, salade de thon	sar-deen, tohn, sah-lad de tohn
Olives, eggs	Olives, oeufs	o-leev, errf
Sugar, honey, salt	Sucre, miel, sel	syew-kr, myel, sel
Preserved meat	Conserve de viande	kohn-serv de vee-ahnd
(Laundry) soap	Savon (à blanchir)	sah-vohn (ah blahn-sheer)
Flour, noodles	Farine, pâtes	fah-reen, paht
Please give me	Donnez-moi, s'il vous plaît	don-nay-mwah, seel-voo-pleh
How much does…cost?	Combien … coûte-t-il?	kohn-byehn … koot-teel?

FRUITS AND VEGETABLES	**FRUITS ET LEGUMES**	**FRWEE AY LAY-GEWM**
Almonds	Amandes	ah-mahnd
Apples	Pommes	pom
Apricot	Abricot	ab-ree-kho
Banana	Bananes	ba-nan
Beans	Haricots	ah-ree-koh
Beetroot	Betterave	bet-rahv
Cabbage	Chou	shoo
Carrot	Carotte	ka-rot
Cauliflower	Chou-fleur	shoo-flerr
Corn	Maïs	mah-ees
Cucumber	Concombre	kohn-kohn-br
Dates	Dattes	dat
Eggplant	Aubergine	oh-ber-zheen
Figs	Figues	feeg
Garlic	Ail	ahy
Grapefruit	Pamplemousse	pahn-pl-moo-ss

Grapes	Raisins	reh-zehn
Lemon	Citron	see-trohn
Lettuce	Laitue	leh-tew
Squash	Courgette	koor-zhet
Melon	Melon	me-lohn
Nuts	Noix	nwah
Onion	Oignons	wahn-yohn
Oranges	Oranges	o-rahnzh
Peaches	Pêches	pesh
Pears	Poires	pwahr
Peas	Petits pois	pe-tee pwah
Pepper	Poivre	pwah-vr
Pomegranate	Grenade	gre-nahd
Potatoes	Pommes de terre	pom-de-tehr
Radish	Radis	rah-dee
Rice	Riz	ree
Spinach	Épinards	ay-pee-nahr
Tomatoes	Tomates	to-maht
Watermelon	Pastèque	pass-tek

BANK	**BANQUE**	**BAHNK**
Where is the nearest bank?	Où est la banque la plus proche?	oo eh la bahnk la plew prosh?
I have dollars to exchange.	J'ai des dollars à changer	zhay des dol-lahr ah shahn-zhay
Travellers checks	Travellers-chèques	travellers-shek
Will you please change... dollars into local currency for me?	Veuillez me changer... dollars en argent local?	ver-yay me shahn-zhay... dol-lahr ahn ar-zhahn lo-kahl
Could I have it in small change, please?	De la petite monnaie, s'il vous plaît	de la pe-teet mo-neh, seel-voo-pleh
... in large notes?	... des grandes coupures	... day grahnd koo-pewr
Could you, please, give me change for this note?	Pouvez-vous faire la monnaie de ce billet, s'il vous plaît?	poo-vay-voo fehr la mo-neh de se bee-yeh, seel-voo-pleh?
Cash, checks	Espèces, chèques	ess-pess, shek
Clerk, manager	Employé, directeur	ahn-plwah-yay, dee-rek-terr
Cash desk, cashier	Caisse, caissier	kess, kess-yay

CLOTHES	**HABITS**	**AH-BEE**
I would like to buy...	Je voudrais acheter ...	zhe vood-reh ash-tay ...
My size is ..., My number is ...	Ma taille est ..., Ma pointure est ...	mah tahy eh ..., mah pwehn-tewr eh ...
May I try it on?	Puis-je l'essayer?	pweezh les-seh-yay?
This is too short, too long	C'est trop court, trop long	seh troh koor, troh lohn
It is too tight, too loose	C'est trop juste, trop large	troh zhewst, troh lahrzh
I would like to have it shortened	Je voudrais le faire raccourcir	zhe vood-reh le fehr rah-koor-seer
A pair of shorts	Pantalon court	pahn-ta-lohn koor
A pair of trousers	Pantalon	pahn-ta-lohn
Boots	Bottes	bot
Brassiere	Soutien-gorge	soo-tyehn-gorzh
Button	Bouton	boo-tohn
Cape	Boléro	boh-lay-roh
Coat	Manteau	mahn-toh
Collar	Col	kol
Cotton material	Cotonnade	ko-to-nahd

Dress	Robe	rob
Gloves	Gants	gahn
Hat	Chapeau	shah-poh
Handkerchief	Mouchoir	moosh-wahr
Jacket	Veste	vest
Ladies' handbag	Sac à main	sack-ah-mehn
Leather	Cuir	kweer
Linen	Lin	lehn
Nylon stockings	Bas de nylon	bah-de-nee-lohn
Night shirt	Chemise de nuit	she-meez de-nwee
Pocket	Poche	posh
Pantyhose	Une paire de collants	ewn pehr de ko-lahn
Pajamas	Pyjama	pee-zhah-mah
Raincoat	Imperméable	ehn-per-may-ah-bl
Robe	Robe	rob
Rubber boots	Bottes en caoutchouc	bot-ahn-kow-choo
Sandals	Sandales	sahn-dahl
Scarf	Écharpe	ay-sharp

Scissors	Ciseaux	see-zoh
Shoe laces	Lacet de chaussures	lah-seh de-shoh-sewr
Shoes	Chaussures	shoh-sewr
Silk	Soie	swah
Skirt	Chemise	she-meez
Slippers	Pantoufles	pahn-too-fl
Sports shoes, sneakers	Chaussures de gymnastique	shoh-sewr de zheem-nass-teek
Stockings	Chaussettes	shoh-set
Sweater	Chandail, pullover	shahn-dahy, pool-oh-vehr
Swimsuit	Maillot de bain	mah-yoh de-behn
Suit	Costume	kos-tewm
Synthetic material	Étoffe synthétique	ay-tof sehn-tay-teek
Belt	Ceinture	sehn-tewr
Tie	Cravate	krah-vat
Umbrella	Culottes	kew-lot
Velvet	Velours	ve-loor
Undershirt, vest	Maillot de corps, gilet	mah-yoh de-kor, zhee-leh
Wool	Laine	len
Zipper	Fermeture éclair	fehr-me-tewr ay-klehr

COLORS

I want a light shade,
- a dark shade
- Red, yellow
- Green, blue
- Purple, gray
- Black, white
- Brown, pink

LAUNDRY

Could you please clean my suit, coat, sweater?

Please could you wash and iron the shirts and underwear for me?

COULEURS

Je voudrais une couleur claire,
- une couleur foncée
- Rouge, jaune
- Vert, bleu
- Violet, gris
- Noir, blanc
- Marron, rose

BLANCHISSERIE

Pouvez-vous nettoyer le costume, le manteau, le pullover, s'il vous plaît?

Pouvez-vous laver et repasser les chemises et les sous-vêtements pour moi?

KOO-LERR

zhe vood-reh ewn koo-lerr
- klehr, ewn koo-lerr fohn-say
- roozh, zhohn
- vehr, bler
- vee-oh-leh, gree
- nwahr, blahn
- mah-rohn, rohz

BLAHN-SHEE-SE-REE

poo-vay-voo net-wah-yay le cos-tewm, le mahn-toh, le pool-oh-vehr, seel-voo-pleh?

poo-vay-voo lah-vay ay re-pass-say lay she-meez ay lay soo-vet-mahn poor mwah?

When will they be ready?	Quand seront-ils prêts?	kahn se-rohn-teel preh?
Please do any necessary repairs	Veuillez repriser ce qu'il faut repriser	ver-yay re-pree-zay se-keel foh re-pree-zay
The belt of the dress is missing	La ceinture de la robe manque	la sehn-tewr de la rob mahnk

AT THE HAIRDRESSER / AU SALON DE COIFFURE / OH SAH-LOHN DE KWAH-FEWR

I want to get a hair cut	Je veux une coupe de cheveux	zhe ver ewn koop de she-ver
In front, on the sides, behind	Frange, les pattes, nuque	frahnzh, lay pat, newk
Shorter, longer	Plus court, plus long	plew koor, plew lohn
Side locks, beard, moustache	Pattes, barbe, moustache	pat, barb, moo-stash
How long must I wait?	Combien de temps dois-je attendre?	kohm-byehn de tahn dwahzh ah-tahn-dr
A short while, a long time	Un petit peu, longtemps	uhn pe-tee per, lohn-tahn
I want a shampoo, please	Je veux un champoing, s'il vous plaît	zhe ver uhn shahn-pwehn, seel-voo-pleh
The water is too hot	L'eau est trop chaude	loh eh troh shohd

I want a shave	Je veux être rasé	zhe ver et-tr rah-zay
Be careful here!	Faites attention ici	fet-zah-tahn-syohn ee-see
I want my hair dyed	Je veux me faire teindre les cheveux	zhe-ver me fehr tehn-dr lay she-ver
I want my hair set	Je veux une mise en plis	zhe verr ewn meez ahn plee
Pedicure, manicure	Un soin de pedicure, un soin de manicure	uhn swehn-de-pay-dee-kewr, uhn swehn-de-mah-nee-kewr

BOOKSHOP / LIBRAIRIE / LEE-BREH-REE

I would like to buy ... — Je voudrais acheter... — zhe vood-reh ash-tay...

- ...a newspaper — ...un journal — ...uhn zhoor-nal
- ...a guidebook — ...un guide — ...uhn geed
- ...a map of the city — ...un plan de la ville — ...uhn plahn de la veel
- ...a map of the country — ...une carte du pays — ...ewn kart dew peh-ee
- ...envelopes — ...des enveloppes — ...day-zahn-vel-lop
- ...a writing pad — ...du papier à lettres — ...dew pap-yay ah let-tr

...an exercise book	...un cahier	...uhn kah-yay
...a pencil	...un crayon	...uhn kreh-yohn
...a fountain pen	...un stylo à encre;	...uhn styee-loh ah-ahn-kr
...a ballpoint pen	...un stylo à bille	....uhn stee-loh ah-bee

WEATHER — LE TEMPS — LE TAHN

What a beautiful day!	Quelle belle journée!	kel bel zhoor-nay
Bright, the sun is shining	Clair, le soleil brille	klehr, le so-lay bree
Warm, hot, very hot	Tiède, chaud, très chaud	tyed, shoh, treh shoh
Chilly, cold, very cold	Frais, froid, très froid	freh, frwah, treh frwah
Dry, heat wave	Sec, vague de chaleur	seck, vahg de shah-lerr
Damp, drizzle, rain	Humide, bruine, pluie	ew-meed, brween, plwee
Cloudy, foggy	Nuageux, brumeux	new-ah-zher, brew-mer
To wear a warm coat	Porter un manteau chaud	por-tay uhn mahn-toh shoh
Raincoat, cape	Imperméable, boléro	ehn-per-may-ah-bl, boh-lay-roh
Rubber boots	Bottes de caoutchouc	bot de-kow-choo
To take an umbrella	Prendre un parapluie	prahn-dr uhn pah-rah-plwee
Parasol	Parasol	pah-rah-sol

TRANSPORT

Bus, train
Underground, express train
Ticket, ticket office

Driver, steward, stewardess

Load/luggage, porter
Where is the lost baggage office?
I left ... in the coach

TRANSPORTS

Autobus, chemin de fer
Métro, train rapide
Billet, bureau de vente de billets

Chauffeur, steward, hôtesse de l'air

Bagages, porteur
Où est le service des objets trouvés?
J'ai laissé ... dans la voiture

TRAHN-SPOR

oh-toh-bews, she-mehn de fehr
may-troh, trehn rah-peed
bee-yeh, bew-roh de vahnt de bee-yeh

shoh-ferr, steward, oh-tess de lehr

ba-gazh, por-terr
oo-eh le sehr-vees day-zob-zheh troo-vay?
zhay leh-say ...dahn la vwah-tewr

TRAIN, BUS

When does the train for ... leave?

TRAINS, AUTOBUS

À quelle heure part le train pour ...?

TREHN, OH-TOH-BEWS

ah kel-err par le trehn poor ...?

How do I get there?	Comment y arriver?	kom-mahn ee-ah-ree-vay?
By train, bus, underground (subway)	En tramway, en autobus, en métro?	ahn-trahn-weh, ahn-noh-toh-bews, ahn-may-troh
At what time does the next train leave for ...?	À quelle heure part le prochain train pour ...?	ah kel-err par le pro-shehn trehn poor ...?
Give me a ticket for ... please	Donnez-moi un billet pour ... s'il vous plaît	don-nay-mwah uhn bee-yeh poor ... seel-voo-pleh
If possible, by the window and facing the front	Si possible, près de la fenêtre et dans le sens de la marche	see poss-see-bl, preh de la fe-net-tr ay dahn le sahn de la marsh
Where can I find a porter?	Où puis-je trouver un porteur?	oo pweezh troo-vay uhn por-terr?
Please, take the bags to the coach	Veuillez mettre les bagages dans le wagon	ver-yay meh-tr lay ba-gazh dahn le vah-gohn
Where is the dining coach?	Où est le wagon-restaurant?	oo eh le vah-gohn-res-tor-rahn?
May I open (close) the window?	Puis-je ouvrir (fermer) la fenêtre?	pweezh oov-reer (fehr-may) la fe-net-tr?

May I smoke?	Puis-je fumer?	pweezh few-may?
When does the train arrive at?	À quelle heure le train arrive-t-il à …?	ah kel-err le trehn ah-reev-teel ah …?
What bus goes to …?	Quel bus va à…?	kel bews vah ah …?
Where is the bus to …?	Où se trouve le bus qui va à…?	oo-se-troov le bews kee vah ah …?
How much is a ticket to …?	Combien coute un billet à …?	kohm-byehn koot uhn bee-yeh ah…?
Is this the bus to …?	Est-ce le bus qui va à …	ess le bews kee vah ah …?
I am looking for this address	Je cherche cette adresse …	zhe shehrsh set ad-ress …
At which station do I get off?	Veuillez me dire où je dois descendre	ver-yay me deer oo zhe dwah des-sahn-dr

AIRPLANE
By which means of transport do I get to the airport?

AVION
Comment puis-je arriver à l'aéroport?

AH-VYOHN
kom-mahn pweezh ah-ree-vay ah la-ay-roh-por?

Is there a bus service (taxi) to there?	Y a-t-il une ligne d'autobus (de taxis) qui y mene?	ee-ah-teel ewn leen-ye doh-toh-bews (de taxi) kee-ee-men?
At what time will I be picked up?	À quelle heure passeront-ils me chercher?	ah kel-err pass-e-rohn-teel me shehr-shay?
Which is the nearest bus stop to the airport?	Quelle est la station la plus proche pour l'aéroport?	kel-eh la stah-syohn la plew prosh poor lah-ay-roh-por?
At what time should I be there?	À quelle heure dois-je être là-bas?	ah kel-err dwahzh et-tr lah-bah?
At what time does the plane take off?	À quelle heure l'avion décolle-t-il?	ah kel-err lah-vyohn day-kol-teel?
Is there a flight to?	Y a-t-il un vol à …?	ee-ah-teel uhn vol ah …?
What is the flight number?	Quel est le numéro du vol?	kel eh le new-may-roh dew vol?
I have nothing to declare	Je n'ai rien à déclarer	zhe nay ryehn ah day-kla-ray
Please, take my luggage	Prenez mes bagages, s'il vous plaît	pre-nay may ba-gazh, seel-voo-pleh

May I have a travel sickness pill, please?	Puis-je recevoir un comprimé contre la nausée?	pweezh re-se-vwahr uhn kohn-pree-may kohn-tr la noh-zay?
May I have a glass of water?	Puis-je recevoir un verre d'eau?	pweezh re-se-vwahr uhn vehr doh?

CAR JOURNEY — VOYAGE EN VOITURE — VWAH-YAZH AHN VWAH-TEWR

Where can I rent a car?	Où puis-je louer une voiture?	oo pweeezh loo-ay ewn vwah-tewr?
I have an international driving license	J'ai un permis de conduire international	zhay uhn per-meëde kohn-dweer ehn-ter-na-syo-nal
How much is it to rent a car per day?	Combien coûte la location d'une voiture pour une journée	kohn-byehn koot la lo-ka-syohn dewn vwah-tewr poor ewn zhoor-nay?
What is the additional rate per kilometer?	Combien dois-je ajouter pour chaque kilomètre de voyage?	kohn-byehn dwazh ah-zhoo-tay poor shack kilometre de vwah-yazh?

Where is the nearest petrol station?	Où se trouve la station d'essence la plus proche?	oo se troov la sta-syohn dess-sahn-ss la plew prosh?
Please, put in ... liters	Je vous prie de mettre ... litres	zhe voo pree de meh-tr ... lee-tr
Check the oil, please	Vérifiez l'huile, s'il vous plaît	vay-ree-fyay lweel, seel-voo-pleh
... the brakes	... les freins	... lay frehn
... the gear box	... la boîte de vitesses	... la bwaht de vee-tess
Please put water in the battery, radiator	Mettez de l'eau dans les accus, le radiateur	met-tay de loh dahn lay-zak-kew, le ra-dee-a-terr
Change the oil in the car, please	Faites les vidanges, s'il vous plaît	fet lay vee-dahnzh, seel-voo-pleh
May I have a road map of the area?	Puis-je avoir une carte des routes de la région?	pweezh a-vwahr ewn kart day root de la ray-zhee-ohn?
Please inflate the tires, the reserve wheel, too	Gonflez les pneus, s'il vous plaît; la roue de secours, aussi, s'il vous plaît	gohn-flay les pner, seel-voo-pleh. la roo de se-koor, oh-see, seel-voo-pleh
Please repair the puncture	Réparez le pneu crevé, s'il vous plaît	ray-pah-ray le pner kre-vay, seel-voo-pleh

English	French	Pronunciation
Please change the inner tube	Changer la chambre à air, s'il vous plaît	shahn-zhay la shahm-br ah ehr, seel-voo-pleh
What is the speed limit?	Quelle est la vitesse permise?	kel-eh la vee-tess pehr-meez?
Which is the way to …?	Quelle est la route pour … ?	kel-eh la root poor …?
Is it a good road?	La route est-elle bonne?	la root eh-tel bon?
Is there a shorter way?	Y a-t-il un chemin plus court?	ee-ah-teel uhn she-mehn plew koor?
Which place is this?	Où nous trouvons-nous?	oo noo troo-vohn-noo?
Is this the road to …?	Est-ce la route pour …	ess la root poor …?
Yes, no	Oui, Non	wee, nohn
Please go back	Marche arrière, s'il vous plaît	marsh ah-ree-ehr, seel-voo-pleh
Go straight on	Continuez tout droit	kohn-tee-new-ay too drwah
Turn to the right (left)	Tournez à droite (à gauche)	toor-nay ah drwaht (ah gohsh)
Turn to the north (south, east, west)	Tournez au nord (sud, est, ouest)	toor-nay oh nor (syewd, est, west)
This way	Voici la route	vwah-see la root
That way	Par cette route	par set root

How far is it to …?	Quelle est la distance jusqu'à?	kel-eh la dee-stahn-ss zhew-skah …
Is it near (far)?	Est-ce près (loin)?	ess preh (lwehn)?
Very far?	Très loin?	treh lwehn?
There, here	Là-bas, ici	lah-bah, ee-see
Please, show me on the map	Montrez-moi la route sur la carte, s'il vous plaît	mohn-tray-mwah la root syewr la kart, seel-voo-pleh
Where are we?	Où sommes-nous?	oo som-noo?
Where is the place that we want to go to?	Où se trouve le lieu où nous devons arriver?	oo-se-troov le-lee-err oo noo de-vohn ah-ree-vay?
On which road should we travel?	Par quelle route devons-nous passer?	par kel root de-vohn noo pa-say?

SIGNS / SIGNES / SEEN–YE

Stop!	Arrêt!	ah-reh!
Caution!	Attention!	ah-tahn-syohn!

Dangerous curve	Courbe dangereuse	koorb dahnzh-rerz
Slow	Lentement	lahnt-mahn
Danger	Danger	dahn-zhay
First Aid	Premier secours	pre-myay skoor
Red Cross	Croix Rouge	krwah roozh
Pharmacy	Pharmacie	fahr-mah-see
Police	Police	po-leess
Fire hydrant	Pompe à incendie	pohmp ah ehn-sahn-dee
No parking	Stationnement interdit	stass-yohn-mahn ehn-tehr-dee
No entry	Entrée interdite	ahn-tray ehn-tehr-deet
No crossing	Défense de traverser	day-fahn-ss de trah-vehr-say
One-way Street	Rue à sens unique	rew ah sahn-ss ew-neek
Pedestrain crossing	Passage pour piétons	pah-sazh poor pee-ay-tohn
Detour	Déviation	day-vee-ah-syohn
Men at Work	Travaux	trah-voh
Right	Droite	drwaht
Left	Gauche	gohsh
Entrance	Entrée	ahn-tray
Exit	Sortie	sor-tee

No Smoking	Défense de fumer	day-fahn-ss de few-may
Information	Informations	ehn-for-mah-syohn
Elevator	Ascenseur	ah-sahn-serr
Restrooms	Toilettes	twah-let
Men	Hommes	om
Women	Femmes	fam
For sale	À vendre	ah vahn-dr
For rent	À louer	ah loo-ay
Travel on this road	Passez par cette route	pass-say par set root
Travel slowly	Allez lentement	ah-lay lahnt-mahn
Take care	Faites attention	fet-zah-tahn-syohn
Crossroad	Chemin de traverse	she-mehn de tra-vehr-ss
Junction, bridge	Jonction, pont	zhohnk-syohn, pohn
Highway, dual highway	Grande route, autoroute à double voie	grahnd root, oh-toh-root ah-doo-ble-vwah
Bad road	Mauvaise route	moh-vez-root
Narrow road	Route étroite	root ay-trwaht
Road under repair	Travaux	trah-voh

Steep incline	Montée raide	mohn-tay red
Steep decline	Pente rapide	pahnt rah-peed
Sharp turn	Virage dangereux	vee-razh dahn-zhe-rer
Blinding light	Lumière aveuglante	lew-mee-ehr ah-verg-lahnt
Children on the road	Passage d'enfants	pass-sazh dahn-fahn

GARAGE / GARAGE / GAH-RAHZH

Is there a garage nearby? — Y a-t-il un garage dans les environs? — ee-ah-teel uhn gah-rahzh dahn lay-zahn-vee-rohn?

Please, check and adjust the brakes — Veuillez vérifier les freins et les ajuster? — ver-yay vay-reef-yay lay frehn ay lay-za-zhew-stay

Please, check the gearbox and adjust the clutch — Veuillez vérifier la boîte de vitesses et l'embrayage? — ver-yay vay-reef-yay la bwaht de vee-tess ay lahm-breh-yazh

The engine uses too much oil — Le moteur consomme trop de l'huile — le mo-terr kohn-som troh de lweel

The engine is overheating — Le moteur chauffe rapidement — le mo-terr shohf rah-peed-mahn

The radiator needs refilling too often	Il manque trop souvent d'eau dans le radiateur	eel mahnk troh soo-vahn doh dahn le ra-dee-a-terr
Please, check the plugs	Veuillez vérifier les bougies	ver-yay vay-reef-yay lay boo-zhee
Please check the points	Veuillez vérifier les platines	ver-yay vay-reef-yay lay plah-teen
The car doesn't start well	La voiture s'allume difficilement	la vwah-tewr sah-lewm dee-fee-seel-mahn
Please, check the headlight alignment	Veuillez vérifier la direction des phares?	ver-yay vay-reef-yay la dee-rek-syohn day fahr
....the wheel balance	...le reglage des pneus	...le reg-lazh day pner

REPAIRS
Oil change
Tighten screws
Fill the radiator

REPACATIONS
Vidanges
Serrer les vis
Mettre de l'eau dans le radiateur

RAY-PAN-RAY-SYOHN
vee-dahnzh
seh-ray les veess
metr de loh dahn le rah-dee-ah-terr

Oil the engine	Mettre de l'huile dans le moteur	metr de lweel dahn le moh-terr
Wheel alignment	Vérifier la direction	vay-reef-yay la dee-rek-syohn
Water for the battery	Eau pour la batterie	oh poor la-bah-te-ree
The gear is stuck	Les vitesses passent mal	lay vee-tess pass mal
...grinding	... grincent	... grehn-ss
The oil is leaking	L'huile fuit	lweel fwee
The part is burnt out	La pièce est abimée	la-pyess eh-tah-bee-may
To take a wheel apart	Démonter le pneu	day-mohn-tay le pner
Short circuit	Court-circuit	koor-seer-kwee
The steering wheel is loose	Il y a du jeu dans le volant	ee-lee-yah dew zher dahn le vo-lahn
Axle rod is broken	L'essieu est cassé	less-yer eh kass-say
Puncture in the tire	Crevaison du pneu	kre-veh-zohn de pner
Everything is O.K.	Tout va très bien	too vah treh byehn

PARTS OF A CAR	**PIÈCES DE L'AUTO**	**PYESS DE LOH-TOH**
Battery	Batterie	bah-te-ree
Brakes	Freins	frehn
Carburetor	Carburateur	kar-bew-rah-terr
Clutch	Embrayage	ahm-breh-yazh
Distilled water	Eau distillée	oh dee-stee-lay
Filter	Filtre	feel-tr
Gear	Boîte de vitesses	bwaht de-vee-tess
Ignition	Allumage	ah-lew-mazh
Lubrication	Lubrification	lew-bree-fee-kah-syohn
Pedal	Pédale	pay-dahl
Piston	Piston	pee-stohn
Radiator	Radiateur	rah-dee-ah-terr
Spark plugs	Bougies	boo-zhee
Spring	Suspension	syew-spahn-syohn
Steering wheel	Volant	vo-lahn
Wheel, wheels	Roue, roues	roo, roo

PHYSICIANS	**MÉDECINS**	**MED-SEHN**
Where does an English speaking doctor live?	Où se trouve un médecin parlant l'anglais?	oo-se-troov uhn med-sehn par-lahn lahn-gleh?
I need first aid	J'ai besoin de soins de première urgence	zhay be-zwehn de swehn de pre-mee-ehr ewr-zhahn-ss
I need an internal specialist	J'ai besoin d'un spécialiste des maladies internes	zhay be-zwehn duhn spay-see-ah-leest day mah-lah-dee ehn-tehrn
Can you recommend a good doctor?	Pouvez-vous me recommander un bon médecin?	poo-vay-voo me re-kom-mahn-day uhn bohn med-sehn?

TYPES OF DOCTORS	**SPÉCIALISTES**	**SPAY-SEE-AH-LEEST**
Ear, nose and throat specialist	Oto-rhino-laryngologiste	oh-toh-ree-noh-lah-rehn-go-lo-zheest
Orthopedist	Orthopédiste	or-toh-pay-deest

Surgeon	Chirurgien	shee-rewr-zhee-ehn
Pediatrician	Pédiatre	pay-dee-atr
Gynecologist	Gynécologue	zhee-nay-ko-log
Dermatologist	Dermatologue	dehr-mah-to-log
Eye specialist	Ophtalmologue	off-tal-mo-log
Neurologist	Neurologue	nerr-roh-log
Internal specialist	Spécialiste des maladies internes	spay-see-a-leest day mah-lah-dee ehn-tehrn
Dentist	Dentiste	dahn-teest

ILLNESSES — MALADIES — MAH-LAH-DEE

I have no appetite	Je n'ai pas d'appétit	zhe-nay-pah dap-pay-tee
Nausea	Nausée	noh-zay
Infection	Infection	ehn-fek-syohn
Depression	Dépression	day-press-yohn
Cold	Rhume	rewm
Vomiting	Vomissement	voh-meess-mahn

Pregnancy, pregnant	Grossesse, enceinte	gro-sess, ahn-sehnt
Contraction	Contraction	kohn-trak-syohn
Heart patient	Cardiaque	kar-dee-ak
Fever	Fièvre	fyeh-vr

PARTS OF THE BODY — PARTIES DU CORPS — PAR-TEE DEW KOR

Ankle	Cheville	she-vee
Appendix	Appendice vermiforme	ah-pahn-dees vehr-mee-form
Arm, artery	Bras, artère	brah, ahr-tehr
Back, bladder	Dos, vessie	doh, vess-see
Blood	Sang	sahn
Bone, bones	Os, os	oss, oh
Breast, chest	Sein, poitrine	sehn, pwah-treen
Ear, elbow	Oreille, coude	oh-ray, kood
Eye, eyes	Oeil, yeux	ehy, yerr
Finger	Doigt	dwah
Foot, feet	Pied, pieds	pyay, pyay

Gland, hand	Glande, main	glahnd, mehn
Head, heart	Tête, coeur	tet, kerr
Heel, hip	Talon, hanche	tah-lohn, ahnsh
Intestine, intestines	Intestin, intestins	ehn-tes-tehn, ehn-tes-tehn
Joint, kidney	Articulations, rein	ar-tee-kew-lah-syohn, rehn
Knee, leg	Genou, jambe	zhe-noo, zhahnb
Ligament, liver	Ligament, foie	lee-gah-mahn, fwah
Lungs, mouth	Poumons, bouche	poo-mohn, boosh
Muscle, neck	Muscle, cou	mew-skl, koo
Nerve, nerves	Nerf, nerfs	nehrf, nehrf
Nose, palm	Nez, paume	nay, pohm
Rib, ribs	Côte, côtes	koht, koht
Shoulder, skin	Épaule, peau	ay-pol, poh
Spine	Colonne vertébrale	ko-lon vehr-tay-bral
Stomach, throat	Estomac, gorge	es-to-mack, gorzh
Thumb, tongue	Pouce, langue	pooss, lahng
Tooth, tonsil	Dent, amygdale	dahn, ah-meeg-dal
Urine, vein	Urine, veine	ew-reen, ven

PHARMACY	**PHARMACIE**	**FAHR-MA-SEE**
Where is the nearest pharmacy?	Où se trouve la pharmacie la plus proche?	oo-se-troov la-fahr-ma-see la plew prosh?
Which pharmacy is on duty tonight?	Quelle est la pharmacie de garde cette nuit?	kel-eh la fahr-ma-see de gard set nwee?
Have you a medicine for a headache?	Avez-vous un médicament pour calmer le mal de tête?	ah-vay-voo uhn may-dee-ka-mahn poor kal-may le mal-de-tet?
Toothache	Mal de dents	mal-de-dahn
Iodine, aspirin	Teinture d'iode, aspirine	tehn-tewr dee-od, as-pee-reen
Valerian drops	Gouttes de valérian	goot-de-vah-lay-ree-ahn
Antiseptic cream	Pommade contre les infections	pom-mahd kohn-tr lay-zehn-fek-syohn
Water bottle, a heating pad	Bouillote, oreiller chauffant	boo-ee-yot, or-ray-yay shoh-fahn
Cottonwool, Band-aid	Ouate, pansement adhésif	waht, pahn-smahn ad-hay-zeef
Thermometer	Thermomètre	tehr-mo-meh-tr

55

TIME	**TEMPS**	**TAHN**
What time is it? It is four o'clock	Quelle heure est-il? Il est quatre heures	kel-err eh-teel? eel-eh katr-err
Five minutes past six, half past five	Six heures cinq, cinq heures et demi	see-zerr sehnk, sehnk-err ay de-mee
A quarter past seven, ten minutes to eight	Sept heures et quart, huit heures moins dix	set-err ay kar, wee-terr mwehn dees
Morning, midday	Le matin, á midi	le ma-tehn, ah mee-dee
Afternoon, evening	L'aprés-midi, le soir	lap-reh-mee-dee, le-swahr,
Night, midnight	La nuit, à minuit	la nwee, ah meen-wee
Today	Aujourd'hui	oh-zhoor-dwee
Yesterday, the day before yesterday	Hier, avant-hier	yehr, ah-vahn-yehr
Tomorrow, the day after tomorrow	Demain, après-demain	de-mehn, ap-reh-de-mehn

A second, hour, quarter of an hour	Une seconde, heure, un quart d'heure	ewn se-kohnd, err, uhn kar-derr
Half an hour, forty minutes	Une demi-heure, quarante minutes	ewn de-mee-err, kah-rahnt mee-newt
Day, days, week, weeks	Jour, jours, semaine, semaines	zhoor, zhoor, se-men, se-men
Month, months, year, years	Mois, mois, année, années	mwah, mwah, ah-nay, ah-nay
Period of ... years	Période de ... ans	pay-ree-od de ... ahn
In a month	Dans un mois	dahn-zuhn mwah
Early, I am early	De bonne heure, je suis en avance	de bon-nerr, zhe swee-zahn-na-vahn-ss
Late, I am late	En retard, je suis en retard	ahn re-tahr, zhe swee-zahn re-tahr

DAYS OF THE WEEK / JOURS DE LA SEMAINE / ZHOOR DE LA SE-MEN

Sunday, Monday	Dimanche, Lundi	dee-mahnsh, luhn-dee
Tuesday, Wednesday	Mardi, Mercredi	mar-dee, mehr-kre-dee
Thursday, Friday	Jeudi, Vendredi	zher-dee, vahn-dre-dee
Saturday	Samedi	sam-dee

MONTHS	MOIS DE L'ANNÉE	MWAH DE LAH-NAY
January, February	Janvier, Février	zhahn-vyay, fayv-ree-ay
March, April, May	Mars, Avril, Mai	marss, av-reel, meh
June, July, August	Juin, Juillet, Août	zhwehn, zhwee-yeh, oo
September, October	Septembre, Octobre	sep-tahm-br, ok-to-br
November, December	Novembre, Decembre	no-vahn-br, deh-sahn-br

SEASONS	SAISONS	SEH-ZOHN
Spring, Summer	Printemps, été	prehn-tahn, ay-tay
Autumn, Winter	Automne, hiver	oh-ton, ee-vehr

NUMBERS	NOMBRES	NOHN-BR
One, two	Un, deux	uhn, der
Three, four	Trois, quatre	trwah, katr
Five, six	Cinq, six	sehnk, seess
Seven, eight	Sept, huit	set, weet
Nine, ten	Neuf, dix	nerf, deess

Eleven, twelve	Onze, douze	ohnz, dooz
Thirteen, fourteen	Treize, quatorze	trehz, kah-torz
Fifteen, sixteen	Quinze, seize	kehnz, sez
Seventeen, eighteen	Dix-sept, dix-huit	dee-set, dee-zweet
Nineteen, twenty	Dix-neuf, vingt	deez-nerf, vehn
Twenty-one, twenty-two	Vingt-et-un, vingt-deux	vehn-tay-uhn, vehn-der
Thirty, forty	Trente, quarante	trahnt, kah-rahnt
Fifty, sixty, seventy	Cinquante, soixante, soixante-dix	sehn-kahnt, swah-sahnt, swah-sahnt-deess
Eighty, ninety, one hundred	Quatre-vingts, quatre-vingt-dix, cent	katr-vehn, katr-vehn-deess, sahn
One hundred and one, two hundred	Cent un, deux cents	sahn-uhn, der-sahn
One thousand, one thousand and one	Mille, mille un	meel, meel-uhn
Two thousand, two thousand and one	Deux mille, deux-mille un	der-meel, der-meel-uhn
One million, one billion	Million, milliard	meel-yohn, meel-yahr

EMERGENCY EXPRESSIONS	EXPRESSIONS D'URGENCE	EX-PRESS-YOHN DEWR-ZHAHNSS
Help!	Au secours!	oh-skoor!
Stop, thief!	Au voleur!	oh vo-lerr!
Leave me alone!	Laissez-moi!	less-say-mwah!
Call the police!	Appelez la police!	ah-play la-po-leess!
I've lost my way.	Je me suis trompé de route.	zhe-me-swee-trohn-pay de root
How do I get to this address?	Comment puis-je arriver à cette adresse!	ko-mahn pweezh ah-ree-vay ah set-ad-ress?
Call me a taxi.	Commandez moi un taxi	ko-mahn-day-mwah uhn taxi
I don't feel well.	Je ne me sens pas bien.	zhe-ne-me-sahn-pah byehn.
Call a doctor!	Appelez le docteur!	ah-play le dok-terr!
Call an ambulance!	Commandez une ambulance!	ko-mahn-day ewn ahn-bew-lahn-ss
Take me to a first-aid station.	Emmenez-moi à la station de premiers secours	ahn-me-nay-mwah ah la stah-syohn de pre-myay skoor.
Take me to the hospital.	Emmenez-moi à l'hôpital.	ahn-me-nay-mwah ah loh-pee-tahl